Then cherish pity, lest you drive an angel from your door.
~ William Blake

Unruly Angels

Diane Buchanan

Frontenac House
Calgary, Alberta

Book and cover design: Epix Design
Cover Image: George Webber
Author photo: Mufty Mathewson

Library and Archives Canada Cataloguing in Publication

Buchanan, Diane (Diane B.)
    Unruly angels / Diane Buchanan.

Poems.
ISBN 978-1-897181-54-6

    1. Drug abuse--Treatment--Poetry. 2. Drug courts--Alberta--Edmonton--Poetry. I. Title.

PS8553.U43333U67 2011   C811'.6   C2011-903232-5

We acknowledge the support of the Canada Council for the Arts for our publishing program. We also acknowledge the support of The Alberta Foundation for the Arts.

 Canada Council for the Arts   Conseil des Arts du Canada    Alberta Foundation for the Arts

Printed and bound in Canada
Published by Frontenac House Ltd.
1138 Frontenac Avenue S.W.
Calgary, Alberta, T2T 1B6, Canada
Tel: 403-245-2491 Fax: 403-245-2380
editor@frontenachouse.com   www.frontenachouse.com

The camera lens not wide enough,
the mike not strong enough
to capture the spirit of this courtroom,
the courage and toughness of the participants,
the empathy and love of the treatment team,
the vision and strength of the Judge.
A camera just won't, it can't—
only an open heart will do.

Acknowledgements

I am indebted to Linda Goyette for so generously giving of her time to read my manuscript at a time when I was questioning its value. Her astute comments, her encouragement and her belief in the importance of such a project motivated me to finish what I had begun.

Many thanks to my other teachers for being so willing to share their expertise and their love of poetry, particularly Shirley Serviss, Patrick Lane, Eunice Scarfe, Sheri-D Wilson, Jannie Edwards and Kate Braid.

My appreciation extends to all of the wonderful women in my two writing groups for their careful listening, insightful suggestions and, always, their interest and support.

I'm grateful to the Edmonton Arts Council for their support.

I want to thank the Drug Treatment Courts of Vancouver, Toronto, Calgary, Regina, Winnipeg, Ottawa and, especially Edmonton, all of whom welcomed me to their courtrooms. Special thanks to Judge Darlene Wong of the Edmonton Drug Treatment and Community Restoration Court for her encouragement from the first poem on.

To the participants, graduates and alumni of Canada's Drug Treatment Courts, these poems are really yours. They are the stories that you generously shared in court each week. They are stories of terrible heartache and tremendous courage. I am grateful to have heard them and to have been able to record them in this way.

I am blessed to be able to share my life with my daughters Ruth, Susan, Meagan, Colleen; my grandson, Matthew; and their families. They are both my roots and my wings.

Finally, to Donald. There are no words to thank you for your constant love and support. Your belief in me and in this project never wavered. We've been travelling life's journey together now for fifty years and I wouldn't have it any other way.

Contents

Foreword

I haven't always lived in the centre of Edmonton. In fact I spent thirty-five years of my life on a horse farm just north of the city where the view from my kitchen window was of mares and foals grazing in white-fenced fields, where the nearest house was miles away, where I could walk alone on country roads, and where I slept to the sound of crickets and coyotes. It was only four years ago that we sold the farm and moved to the city and the homeless became my neighbours. They begged on the streets where I walked and they slept on park benches and in doorways. Home for one man was a large cardboard box that sheltered his dingy belongings in the ravine just beyond our condominium's recycle bin. Another couple lived in the backyard of an empty building next door. From my kitchen window I would often see another woman struggle to push her grocery cart of belongings up a steep hill from the river valley. At night I could hear their drunken voices, police sirens and on a few occasions, gun shots. One morning as I walked past a small park I noticed a very ragged and bedraggled individual sprawled apparently lifeless across the stairs of a gazebo. It occurred to me that he might have died there and nobody, including me, was brave enough to check. It was quite a relief when he finally moved an arm. The homeless lived here and so did I. I could no longer just leave the problem behind as I drove home away from the city.

I don't know the statistics and I know that not all homeless people are addicts, but I suspect that having an addiction could certainly lead to being homeless. It probably works the other way too, particularly for young people who are forced to leave abusive situations and find themselves on the street. Hunger and addiction often lead to crime. In the Edmonton Journal recently the commissioner of federal prisons was quoted as saying that four out of five prisoners who enter federal penitentiaries have substance abuse problems and fifty per cent committed their crimes under the influence of drugs, alcohol or other intoxicants. Now I was coming face to face with this problem daily.

The man accosted my husband and me outside the restaurant where we'd just had brunch one Sunday morning. He demanded money, cursing loudly as he staggered beside us, insulting, accusing, and threatening.

His ragged shirt was torn open and hanging off his arms, his hair was ratted and mangy and there was a large wet patch in the crotch of his jeans. He wouldn't leave us alone until my husband got out his cell phone to call the police, at which time he disappeared down the stairs of the LRT station.

The homeless problem had become personal. It appeared to be growing and there seemed to be no solutions. Then one day a small article in the Edmonton Journal caught my attention: *Drug court gives addicts hope.* I was already familiar with the Court House as I'd written *Between the Silences*, a collection of poetry about Youth and Family Court, in 2005, but I hadn't been back since. So, after almost four years' absence, I went back to sit in on a Wednesday afternoon in Courtroom 267. I found poems there! Not grand or flowery, no, these poems were like the tiny brown birds that flutter in the underbrush—life's understory—often trampled on and ignored, but oh, so curious and surprisingly sublime.

Hard to forget that frail waif of a girl, abused by her stepfather, on the streets at fourteen, an addict by fifteen, today bouncing to the front of the courtroom at thirty to speak about her six months of being clean, and how she was keeping busy painting her mother's fence. The mother she hadn't spoken to in fifteen years. And I'll always remember the young man with that small dagger sticking out between his nose and upper lip, who in his first appearances had seemed a hopeless case. Six months later, with jeans hung so low over his boxer shorts he had to hold them up, he proudly told the court how he went to sixty meetings in sixty days. And the mother, an elder in her tribe who was there from the first time her daughter, a beautiful woman with long straight black hair, appeared in the prisoner's dock to her daughter's graduation day, when she presented the Judge with flowers.

It's been said that Drug Treatment Court is the most significant criminal justice initiative in a century. It's a court specifically designed to supervise cases of drug dependant offenders who have agreed to accept treatment for their addiction. The first Drug Court was initiated in 1989 in Florida. There are, at latest count, 2,559 drug courts operating in the United States, and it is estimated that they will serve over 120,000 people. Internationally there are drug courts in Europe, South America, the Caribbean, New Zealand and Australia. There are six federally funded drug courts in Canada: Toronto, Vancouver, Ottawa, Winnipeg, Regina, and Edmonton. Other cities have begun to recognize the value of drug courts and are finding ways to establish and fund their own. For instance Calgary is funded mainly by the City of Calgary, while the Durham Drug Treatment and Mental Health Court in Ontario depend on the court, lawyers, mental health professionals, police and other members of the team to donate their time and resources. At last count there were eleven drug courts operating in Canada.

All these drug courts work in partnership with the criminal justice system, drug addiction treatment services, social service agencies and the community. Their goal is to save lives and, in the process, reduce the individual, social and economic cost of illicit substance abuse, the crimes associated with it and the resulting incarceration.

The Edmonton Drug Treatment and Community Restoration Court began on December 7, 2005 as a two year trial, on a limited budget with one Judge and a treatment team ready to try this new way to solve an age old problem. They developed their own mission statement based on the same principles as all of the drug treatment courts but which also incorporated the principles of restorative and community justice. While this Court does not provide direct treatment services as some of the others do, it has a unique, highly individualized treatment approach in which the treatment team and the participant develop a treatment plan together.

I began to look forward to Wednesday afternoons. It is a fifteen-minute walk from my place to the courthouse, through security, up one floor to Courtroom 267, where I take my usual seat in the back row. There's a different atmosphere in this courtroom: upbeat, the lively buzz of participants mixed with the silent tension of those three, four, sometimes up to seven people in custody, dressed in navy prison garb and perched on a straight wooden bench, fenced in and surrounded by stern, armed security guards. It's a mixed group, male and female, young and old, tattooed, pierced, scarred, bearded, clean cut, some overweight, some gaunt and, sadly, too often, some pregnant. There are those who are here for the first time to observe and those who are already on the ever-present waiting list.

They are all adults who have met certain credibility criteria. They have outstanding charges related to their drug dependence but none of these involve commercial drug trafficking, violence, children or gang associations. Their sentences are not expected to exceed three years. They must be motivated to change their behaviour and ready to commit to a minimum of one year in the Drug Treatment program to do so.

The prisoner J. startled me when he first began to speak to the Judge. It was not only the rich low tone of his voice but also the clarity and depth of his language. He'd be in his late forties I guessed, tall and lean with brown hair that was thinning at the front so that he was left with a wide, shiny brow. He seemed so out of character dressed in those faded institutional overalls, standing at attention in the prisoner's dock and talking so fluently to the Judge, each word articulated with an inflection that was both impressive and humble. "I'm basically homeless," he confesses. "I was a plumber. I've lost it all, my wife, my home, my tools. I have many regrets."

"This is a new beginning for you," says the Judge. "Don't let me down."

Participation in the Drug Treatment Program is voluntary. The participants must plead guilty to their crimes and are released on strict bail conditions until sentencing that occurs after completion of the program. The program requires intensive participation and there are many conditions—including, in Edmonton, that they come to court every Wednesday afternoon to report to the Judge. This meant that I saw the same people every week. They didn't know me, although I must have become a familiar question mark to some, but it wasn't long before I knew their faces and their stories. Drug Court was changing my attitudes, my concerns. It was changing me.

Weekly, I listen to J. as he talks to the Judge; first about the six weeks he spent at a residential intensive addiction treatment centre, then about his mother, who is ill in the United States. How he wishes he could go to her, how he'd like to ask for her forgiveness, how much he regrets his past life. Later he talks of fixing up his residence, then beginning to work again, how he must climb sixteen flights of stairs in a building under construction, how he confesses to having relapsed the night he heard his mother died, how he immediately phoned his probation officer, how he told the truth, how sorry he is …

The foundation for participation is honesty and personal engagement. Relapses happen and, if the participant is honest and admits to having used, there are no sanctions imposed.

One of the first steps in the Edmonton Drug Rehabilitation Court Program is mandatory attendance at either a residential or outpatient intensive addiction treatment centre for approximately six weeks, after which clients move back into the community, subject to the strict conditions of their probation. These conditions prescribe where they can reside, who they can see, specific areas to avoid, strict curfews, weekly screens of urine, saliva or blood for drugs, regular attendance at addiction meetings such as Alcoholics Anonymous, participation in courses offered by the Drug Treatment

Court, completion of community volunteer hours as well as weekly attendance at court to report to the Judge. The Drug Court team and the participant work together to create a long-term individualized treatment, recovery and reintegration plan. After a year the individual may apply to graduate and, if successful, the participant receives a non-custodial sentence upon graduation.

J. is dressed in a dark suit, white shirt, red tie and black oxfords the day he graduates. There is no immediate family present but you wouldn't know it. The courtroom is filled with his friends. He is poised and articulate as usual, though emotional as he thanks the court and the team. Finally he singles out two men in particular who had helped him. The first had taken him for coffee when he found him panhandling outside a Mac's store. This man had cared enough to stay in touch, supply warm clothes and food, came to visit him in jail. The second man had given him a place to live while he was in rehabilitation, drove him to meetings, found him a job. He's been clean for almost a year, has a place to live, a job, friends and the drug court alumni group to support him. A new life, a new beginning, a reason to celebrate.

I wanted to see how other drug courts worked so I organized a visit to Vancouver's Drug Court. To get there I had to drive down East Hastings Street. I had heard that Vancouver has a big drug problem but nothing could have prepared me for what I saw. I realized that this was just the tip of the iceberg and a warning for other communities. Addiction to drugs and alcohol was increasing everywhere. Something had to be done, and Drug Treatment Courts that offer rehabilitation instead of incarceration are one answer, a second chance for the addict and new found hope for families and communities. Drug Court is one way to break the cycle of addiction, which leads to crime that leads to incarceration, and incarceration and release without treatment lead right back to addiction, crime, punishment and on and on and on around the cycle.

The Toronto Drug Treatment Court began in 1998 and was the first of its kind in Canada. It is held in a stately old building called "Old City Hall". Once through security I was dwarfed as I stepped into the foyer with thirty-foot ceilings, marble floors, gilded columns, stained glass windows and a very large, ornate divided staircase. Into this eroded opulence step the participants of Toronto's Drug Court every Tuesday and Thursday. I visited one warm spring Thursday afternoon. Although there were many similarities I was interested and pleased to meet a court-appointed peer counsellor, an early graduate of the Toronto Drug Court program and, also, the courthouse Chaplain. They work alongside the Drug Court team to assist the participants. Although every Drug Court differs depending on the jurisdiction, the demographics and the social conditions, they all work with one basic concept: to blend the traditional processes of the criminal justice system with those of the drug treatment community. Drug Treatment Court works wherever it exists. I witnessed it again first hand that day in Toronto.

It is graduation day for this tall handsome black man. He's come straight from work at a construction job dressed in bright yellow coveralls still wearing the vest with a big X on the back. "Can't miss you today," says the Judge, greeting him with a smile. "What can you tell these people here to help them get to where you are?"

"Out of sight, out of mind," he responds turning around to face the audience. "I got out of downtown, away from those familiar places, familiar faces. I moved. Then I met a wonderful woman who only knew me when I was clean. I'm getting married next year. I got a job and a future now. Thanks to this court I've begun again, got a new life."

Where Toronto meets in the antiquated surroundings of another era, Calgary's drug treatment court meets in a futuristic tower of metal and glass.

While most of the other drug treatment programs in Canada are funded by the federal government, Calgary's Court was able to open in May, 2007 thanks to a funding initiative by the City of Calgary. The Alberta government now funds this court, at least temporarily. At the moment their program is capped at sixteen participants whose average length of stay is fourteen months. The day that I visited they celebrated their fifth graduation from the program. Almost all the participants that day were able to take a "trip to the bucket" where perfect compliance with the program requirements and a clean drug test are rewarded with a coffee card, chocolate or a movie pass. When a participant proudly announces the number of days clean from drugs there is loud applause. I was impressed with the relaxed, friendly atmosphere. Certainly on that day there was a feeling of optimism and hope that spread from the graduate and his family to the rest of us in that courtroom.

Regina's Drug Treatment Court has been in operation since 2006 and, like Vancouver, runs a day-patient rehabilitation program out of their centre. Participants are required to attend from 9am to 4pm Monday to Friday with the exception of Tuesday afternoon, when they appear in court to report to the presiding Judge. While the basic philosophy of each Drug Court is the same, there are certainly differences in the way the program is managed, determined, I suspect, by the availability of support systems such as long term residential rehabilitation and housing facilities for both men and women in the area. But the one constant has been the dedication of the members of the Drug Court team, and certainly Regina is no different in this regard.

The Winnipeg and Edmonton Drug Treatment Courts seem to be the most alike. Both have been in operation for over five years and both can boast of almost fifty successful graduates from the program.

Like the city itself, Ottawa's Drug Treatment Court was a little more formal, with the participants sitting on one side, the team and visitors on the other. Still, the atmosphere in the courtroom was relaxed and there was praise and encouragement for successful participants in the form of coffee cards and early release for the day.

In his book *In The Realm of Hungry Ghosts* Gabor Maté writes, "Drug addicts are often dismissed and discounted as unworthy of empathy and respect. In the dark mirror of their lives, we can trace outlines of our own." In my experience, empathy and respect underlie every part of the Drug Court program. I have been sitting in on the Edmonton Drug Treatment Court for almost four years. I find it to be a place of optimism, humour and hope. I've witnessed anger, sorrow, fear and incredible courage. I've joined in with the rest of the courtroom to applaud reports of clean screens, I've worried about those who didn't appear, was saddened when warrants were issued, or people were put back into custody. I've wept at relapses, rejoiced at successes and celebrated at a more than few graduations. I've seen mothers reunited with their children, young people with their families, husbands with their wives and healthy babies born to young women. I've laughed and cried right along with the rest of the courtroom. I've watched and admired the empathy of the treatment team, the patience of the Judge, the courage of the participants, the camaraderie of the alumni and the wonderful way that they all support each other. I believe they are serving a very important function in our community. Lives are being changed. People are being saved. Drug Court is helping people break out of that malignant cycle of addiction.

S. reminded me of my daughters when I first saw her. She was young, pretty, with long blond hair swept up in a ponytail. She kept her head down, her shoulders rounded as she nervously played with her sweats. When her name was finally called she had to pull herself up using the rail of the prisoners box and I knew from the roundness under those navy sweats that there was more than one life to be concerned with here.

My presence in this court is not simply to be a spectator. Carolyn Forché writes about a Poetry of Witness which, she suggests, is neither personal nor political but somewhere in between in a space she calls: "the social; a place of resistance and struggle … By situating poetry in this social space we can avoid some of our residual prejudices … In fact, the poem might be our only evidence that an event has occurred … Poem as trace, poem as evidence."

Fifteen months later I am there when S. graduates. She's holding her blond, curly haired daughter, a healthy, happy nine-month old. Her mother thanks the court for giving her daughter back, explains how grateful their family is to have their beautiful granddaughter. S. is a woman now, poised and confident. She's gone back to school. She has a goal. She wants to become a physician. She wants to help other women who, like her, have been seduced by the lure of crystal meth.

Gabor Maté says, "No society can understand itself without looking at its shadow side …" I believe that it is time to look at this shadow side of our society, that there is a place for a Poetry of Witness in the Drug Treatment Courts of Canada—not about the "war on drugs" but about the people who have found themselves caught in its crossfire and have found a "truce position". In Drug Treatment Court there is a new reason for hope.

Short Circuit

Trying to Write a Poem While Driving Down East Hastings Street on the Way to Observe in Vancouver's Drug Treatment Court

This poem can't shape itself
around this writhing mass of human
beings outside the car, can't
begin to find a metaphor to describe all
the barred doors, broken windows,
empty buildings, nameless businesses, can't
separate the garbage from the hand beneath
a pile of newspapers or the sock foot
wiggling through the hole in a black
plastic bag, can't find an image
beyond the sirens, flashing lights,
paddy wagon, paramedics rolling
a limp body onto a stretcher.

This poem festers with broken boils,
scabies, lice, vomit, sewer water
injected into veins,
lies dull and lifeless on sidewalks,
in doorways and dumpsters,
sleeps with the devil, disease, death.

This poem is a cigarette butt, bent
needle, sodden quilt, broken bottle,
empty syringe, ripped condom.
It is too heavy to carry,
yet it has latched on, won't let go,
speaks in tongues, ululates
across a desert of shattered bones,
shattered hearts, souls, lives.

This poem wants to hope, searches
dilated pupils, unfocused eyes,
drooped heads, down-turned mouths,
flaccid bodies, slippery hands.

This poem can't ignore
that young woman in soggy boots,
ragged mini skirt, skimpy top, one hand
glued to the handle of a shopping cart,
tattooed body folded right over
straw hair sweeping the sidewalk.
It wants to look the other way
doesn't want to demean, wants to show
respect, wants these human beings
to have some dignity where
there is none.

This poem is somebody's daughter,
son, mother, father, uncle, aunt, cousin,
somebody's somebody, searching
for something, some-thing, some thing.
It is a roiling sea
of drug-soaked decay, a Tarot card
warning, a tsunami presage.

This poem will die unnamed,
unclaimed. It reeks
of urine, sweat, stale beer,
and shit, which makes it hard
to understand, not enough music,
too much horror, all of the images
decomposed, the story disjointed,
too many lives shortened, too many
deaths, too many, just too much. It's
just too much.

But this poem has to because
some poem has to. So it will
wrap its scarred and scrawny lines
around that golden elm tree
in Pigeon/Needle Park and
                    pray.

All Rise

~ a found poem

These two simple words instil a sense of awe and respect
in the courtroom, demand everyone leap to attention.

In Drug Court they have even greater meaning.
Here addicted people receive life-changing treatment.

Instead of indifference they are shown compassion,
instead of judgement they are given assistance,

instead of punishment they are provided
a passport to recovery.

All Rise captures the essence of what a Drug Court does,
how it provides hope to those labelled hopeless.

It's a promise made to help every participant
recognize the good in themselves,

a commitment to look beyond the chaos and wreckage,
to see their humanity, value and future.

Those two words call attention to the countless
who have proven recovery is possible.

All Rise renews the conviction
that no case is beyond reach.

For, when one person rises out of drugs and crime,
we *All Rise.*

Why Use?
~ a found poem

First

to feel
good

Then

to feel
better

Finally

to feel
n
  o
    t
      h
        i
          n
            g
              at
                all

The Circuit

1.

helplessly
running
from the great darkness
she is reaching out
grasping for the nearest hand
closing her eyes
under yesterday's dress
brutal tattoos of plum and wine
her bare feet numb
in the muck of the street
she drinks toxic water
to quench her aching thirst
her body still yearns for light
and yet she knows
in this night there is no light
the bulb is cracked
she is caught
charged caged whipped broken
ejected and rejected again
she loathes her manacled mind
as she circles
inside that great bruised darkness
running
out of time

2.

out of time
running
inside that great bruised darkness
as he circles
he loathes his manacled mind
ejected and rejected again
charged caged whipped broken
he is caught
the bulb is cracked
in this night there is no light
and yet he knows
his body still yearns for light
to quench his aching thirst
he drinks toxic water
in the muck of the street
his bare feet numb
brutal tattoos of plum and wine
under yesterday's boots
closing his eyes
grasping for the nearest hand
he is reaching out
from the great darkness
running
helplessly

Addiction

~ Inspired by Elizabeth Tomes' Sleep

First you must *name* it, *say* it, *own* it. But only when you are ready to do so on your knees, only if you will allow yourself to be wrapped in swaddling clothes, only if you can see yourself wearing them like a flag as you enter the tunnel to sobriety. If you expect to escape from your addiction by taking a short hike on a summer day, you'll find yourself running a marathon under thundering skies. Expect peace, like an empty chapel or a still pond to take you on: you'll find yourself clinging to a driftwood cross on a rain-tossed lake.

Leave those steel-toed boots behind. Walk barefoot, feel the earth beneath you. Allow yourself to be lead through the darkest muck of the tunnel. Replace the divots you've made but keep moving. Count to twelve; do it, again, and again, and again. Focus on that small marble of light ahead until your addiction becomes a scar on your heart, a constant reminder to offer your hand to those who stumble around you on your day-to-day clamber to find your own luminous life, to swim with the dolphins.

The Empty Chair

     Dead
he was
found
dead
yesterday
scuttlebutt said
          overdose
his legacy
     left
in their heads
       this—
knowing
that it could
have been
any one
of them
     dead

The Addict's Mask

There are in this world a lot of devils with wondrous
smiles. Also, many unruly angels. ~ Mary Oliver

What lies hidden behind that mask
frozen with such a wondrous smile
the first time they appear in court,
on a last minute reprieve from jail?

Do they mar their image after being read
a cascade of conditions, when they quibble
over curfews, cell phones, community service hours?

Do they want to change with every bone of their being,
desperate for help to tame their compulsive nature,
or are they seeking to escape
under Drug Court's umbrella?

Are those weekly conversations with the Judge
just rote, a jovial treacle of empty words,
a way to save face?

Or, are they ready to remove that mask,
look into the mirror, face their demons,
reveal, however unruly,
the terrified angel inside?

What Is This Place?

What Is This Place?

This place of last resort;
this windowless, fluorescent-lit, oak-bound place,
with podium, lectern, pews and locks, even
a prisoners box, this second-floored, double-doored,
security-laced, self-effaced, customary,
ordinary courtroom.

This place is aimed at addicts, with a shot
at recovery. They say you could do
two years in jail easier
than coming here. You must really want it,
really want to do it, really want to fight,
must want to change, want to be here,
in this court, want to go through it,
all those Wednesday afternoons, clean screens,
AA and NA meetings, curfews, sanctions, conditions,
permissions, restrictions. It's not for everyone,
this challenging, remarkable, atypical,
exceptional courtroom 267.

Wanted:

A double-headed eagle
for this courtroom, double-
headed, double-minded,
a dual approach to this affliction
of addiction. Add a double

pair of eyes, sharp, clear, wise
one pair to view what is,
the obvious, the self-
evident. The other

must be keen enough
to gaze upon the heavens
of the mind—
to grasp the hell.

For only the eagle can
fly above the storm, see
what lies ahead, look
into the sun without blinking.

Only she.

Drug Treatment Court

~ a found poem

Ground-breaking,
nothing like the usual sombre court room.
Addicts hope here.
Treatment offered ahead of jail.
There is laughter, loud applause and hugs.
Wednesday, a young woman smiled,
after she had just pleaded guilty, said *thank you*
as she was led back into custody. The Judge replied
we look forward to hearing from you.
Nothing like the usual, except—
too few staff, too few beds and
a backlog of addicts.

Pre-Court Meeting

It's confidential, a covert operation
in the basement of the courthouse,
happens at high noon
though one can only speculate
about the where's and what's and how's
of this secret session where fates
are determined behind closed doors.

Does admittance require a password,
secret handshake, special key? Are cards
or dice involved? Does one bring food
to the séance, brew to the coven, sweet grass
for the powwow? Could it be
a Ouija board is used to determine the future
of that last addict to fall from grace?

The Choice

Hugs or handcuffs,
this probation officer prescribes
both. Choose the first
and you'll receive a good supply
as long as you carefully follow the conditions
on the label. It's given freely
to those who really want to heal. Take
as many as necessary to relieve the pain.
Know it's not a cure but it does help
relieve the symptoms. Works best
when mixed with honesty. Could be fatal
if taken while swallowing a lie.

Shoes

*Fit us with boots to suit our own feet and make us tolerant
of the footgear of the rest.* ~ Emily Carr

boots, sandals, wedgies, pumps
with pointed toes and sling back heels,
moccasins, running shoes, even slippers,
this treatment case-manager carries
all kinds of footwear in her briefcase.

Be prepared, her motto, always be ready
to walk with your clients no matter how rocky
the path, how steep the climb—
just as long as you both can agree
on the destination.

A Cynical Man

They say I'm a cynical man. Hard
not to be for a security guard
handling these lousy prisoners all day,
not the cream of the crop, you know, these
criminals: thieves, prostitutes, addicts,
problem people, the dregs, finally they got caught,
arrested, charged, jailed. Now
they're in my custody. My job today,
to herd them in and out of this courtroom
without commotion.

It's the same ones, you know, over and over,
in for a while, a few good meals, warm bed,
a shave or two and then they're right back
on the street, back on the dope, back doing whatever
it takes to get high. I know they'd crush me
if they ever got the chance. I've heard it all, seen it all,
been kicked and bit, sworn and spit at more times
than I can count. Got no patience left for these
goddamned addicts.

Yeah I'm a cynical man, who wouldn't be.
Badged and uniformed, armed, radio attached,
putting on or taking off handcuffs,
unlocking or locking up, moving these surly slugs
from one cell to another. Always wary.
One never knows when
you deal with losers.

Never been to Drug Court before. I managed
to avoid those Wednesdays in 267—
until now. Not my choice to spend
my afternoon in a courtroom full of addicts.
Can't imagine any good could come of this.

Yet, it's different here, the atmosphere,
seems to be one of hope, not despair and
there's laughter,
and, well, they do seem
so ordinary.

Like, take this young guy
who's graduating today. I've seen him before
behind bars, almost didn't recognize him
all clean and shaved, dressed in suit and tie.
He tells the court he's going back to school,
plans to become a doctor. Wants to help
other addicts. He even thanks the Judge
for ordering him to go for drug rehabilitation.
That's like thanking the doctor
for your rectal examination!

Then, would you believe, that same Judge,
well, she gets up from her seat,
makes her way down the stairs, gown and all,
goes to front of the courtroom
just to give him a hug? I'm concerned
for her safety but nobody moves, they just clap.
Some even wipe away tears. Not me.

Funny, as I direct my prisoners
from the courtroom back to their cells
they seem different. It's like I see them
as people, you know, like you and me. Maybe
here in this courtroom there is hope—
even for a drug addict.

Intersection

He came just before Drug Court began,
a good looking, clean cut young man,

late twenties maybe, the same age
as some of those present today,

could have been one of them, except
for the wire in his ear,

the shadow of a bulletproof vest
beneath his dark blue uniform,

the holstered gun at his hip,
the EPS crest on his shoulder.

He's probably arrested a few in the pews today,
most look away, avoid eye contact, sit elsewhere,

until they're encouraged to meet him,
let him explain his reason for coming.

He's heard their stories,
seen how they're changing their lives.

He's come to commend them, to give
each a coffee card, a smile, to offer his hand.

He could have been one of them, same age, yet—
his path took him one way, theirs another.

What made the difference doesn't matter anymore,
for today the policemen and the addict

have met at an intersection. From here
the road they choose is up to them.

The Alumni of Drug Treatment Court

They've set the bar high,
this exclusive group,
whose members have walked
over hot coals and survived. They've
earned the right to belong.

They're giving
not taking,
making
not breaking,
restoring,
not scoring,
healing,
not stealing,
paying off,
paying back, paying—
                    taxes!

They ladle soup to the homeless,
pack boxes at the food bank,
cook for Meals on Wheels,
set up chairs at church,
fix toys,
play Santa at Christmas.

They shovel your snow,
mow your lawns,
bake your bread,
move your furniture,
wait tables, take tickets,
stack, wrap and pack groceries,
drive taxis, trucks, buses.

They plumb, plaster, paint,
cut hair, clean house, make music
design computer programs,

go back to school—
someday
they could be your personal trainer, massage therapist,
yoga instructor, counsellor, nurse, doctor—

                                        someday

It takes guts to want to change,
to admit your addiction, put that life
and those friends behind you,
to meet all the strict conditions,
to be screened on demand,
come to court weekly to sit
all afternoon for a two minute report. To attend
AA meetings, anger management classes,
do community service hours for a year.
To hold your head up when you apply
for work with a record.

Alumni don't have to come back.
They've done their time, earned
their right to freedom, yet still
they come, proud and often,
happy to talk, happy to report their progress,
happy to applaud a clean screen,
to encourage, educate and welcome.
They are the backbone of the program.

Their past—their ghost,
their future—their hope,
their future—our hope.

This Place You Call Drug Court

It will not line your path with rose petals.
It will not provide cushions.
It will not promise a smooth ride.
It will not erase the scars you carry
from that fall you endured as a child
in the bush behind the barn.
It will not abide time shovelling manure.
It will not make your bed, will not
wash your dirty laundry, will not
clean under your fingernails.
It will not hide the keys
to that wooden box of dreams
you buried as a teen.
It will not read your tea leaves,
your palm or your aura.
It will not run your bath or scratch
the itch you cannot reach.
It will not tar and feather.
It will not burn incense to disguise
the scent of baby sweat and leather.
It will not euthanize, baptize or circumcise.
It will not supply extra bones for backs.
It will not bend for forked tongues.
It will not put pins in dolls. No hex. No sex.
It will not be your lover.
It will not say *Never*.

It may snort and kick, even buck
you off a few times, but—
it will give you another leg up,
and, when you've got that sucker tamed—
it will lead you to a fresh starting gate.

Courtroom Waltz

A Familiar Face in an Unfamiliar Place

You might have seen him before, or,
someone just like him, red eyed,
skinny, toothless, unshaven, unkempt,
looking for a handout outside
any Mac's store on any city street.

You're almost certain you've seen him before,
but not here in this courtroom, not clean,
not sober, not dressed in prison sweats,
talking to the Judge, asking for help
for his addictions. A meek old man.

You're sure you've seen him before
when he pleads guilty
to conveying open liquor
on the street, guilty to harassing
and jostling pedestrians.

Yes, you've seen him before. He's the one
we try to ignore, the one we're afraid of,
too dirty, too hungry, too drunk.
We lock up bathrooms in stores,
turn him away at the door, call the police.
He's the one sleeping in the park defenceless
against bullies and hoodlums. Stoned.

You've seen him before, but this time
you see a person sick with an addiction.
You feel his defeat. You see vulnerability
in his eyes, and now, perhaps, even a hint
of hope as the Judge releases him
into the Drug Treatment Program.

He's to go to a recovery centre,
report back to court once a week, take
drug screening tests, join AA, stay away
from alcohol, drugs and that Mac's store.

*This is your chance to learn how to live
straight and clean*, says the Judge.
You know you've seen him, or
someone just like him, before. You know
you will never look at him the same way again.

The Note

Shiny new running shoes carry his scrawny body
to the front of this drug treatment court. Shoulders
drooped, eyes lowered, the young man
takes a crumpled note from his back pocket,
hands it to the solemn Judge:

> *I didn't want to come today. Had another lapse.*
> *My cravings got the best of me, I didn't ask for help,*
> *didn't talk to anyone, didn't think, just went and used.*
>
> *Today is an anniversary of sorts. Two months*
> *I've spent in a bed, two months with a foam pillow*
> *instead of a rolled magazine under my head.*
>
> *I don't want to go back, back to that place*
> *in the bush by the river, back to that tent, back to*
> *the fear, the hunger, the cold, I couldn't face that.*
>
> *It's all out on the table now, the stealing, the using,*
> *the lying. No place left to run, no place*
> *to hide, no place for deception here. It's time to repent.*
>
> *There's too much at stake. I'm bound*
> *by this court's conditions, want to end this torment,*
> *kick my old habits, turn over a new leaf.*
>
> *No more tent, tarp or grocery cart.*
> *No more smoking, sniffing or shooting up.*
> *I'd like the chance to learn how to live differently.*
>
> *Never knew my father, my mother overdosed,*
> *my hockey coach—indecent. I was only ten.*
> *I've been on the streets since then.*

"Etiolates" my doctor told me, that's what heroin does,
you lose energy, wilt, like a plant without light. Prescribed
methadone to slake this gnawing need.

I don't want to waste another day
of my life. I promise, I intend to follow
all your orders. I'll find a way. Please let me stay.

With your help, I know I can get a grip on this.
I've got to find the grit to quit. I know I can
'cause I don't ever want to go back to that tent again.

Games

Your Honour I don't think I'm being dishonest. I told the drug treatment team about my pain how I just had to see a doctor how he'd prescribed something. I told them even before that piss test showed up positive. I told them I'd taken that pill just thirty minutes before the test.   What?   Opiates wouldn't show up that soon?   Well maybe it was an hour before, could have been more, I don't really remember, but that Doctor he prescribed them for me.   I sure won't go back there again. You see they made me wait so long and the pain got so bad, well I just had to had to take one   just one of my mom's pills from the bottle of Tylenol, ones I bought over the counter last week at the drugstore for her.   Yeah they were for her. You see she gets really bad headaches so with the pain and all I just had to take one of hers. Yes one.   Well maybe it might have been more before I finally got in to see that doctor. Yeah he knew about my addiction.   This program? Well I think he knew. He should have known. I'll tell you I sure won't go back there again. They don't know nothin'.   You know now that I think about it I could have taken another pill earlier that morning. Maybe that was what caused the bad screen   or maybe I took two I can't recall   but I told them I took something,   I have trouble remembering these days.   Overwhelmed.   Too much to do. I need a new doctor. I'm never goin' back to him. But really I did confess. I don't think I'm being dishonest …

Wanted: A New I.D.

How do you control your anger
when it has shaped you, become
your armour, that tough guy demeanour,
all thistle skinned, with bullet words
and shotgun fists?

How do you separate
that shadow from the man
when you believe that fury
is who you are, fed
for so long on drugs,
street-fights, cage-matches?

How do you even begin
to wrap your skin around
all that rage now you're clean,
trying hard to go straight?

How do you dampen
those embers of hate
that smoulder in your gut,
when you know it would
only take a tiny flurry
for them to flare up,
become you again?

Today you tell the Judge you're scared,
scared of your anger, it's grown,
bigger than you, too hard
to smother. You swallow
flames, tell her you're sorry,
sorry about last week, the lashing out,
the intimidation. That's not who you are
any more, you say, it's not
who you want to be ...

      How can you know who you want to be now,
      when you've always been Anger
      fired into the shape of a man?

The Procrastination Paper

He reports he was late for work a few times last week,
confused by his twenty-four-hour clock,
passes wrinkled pages to the Judge,
a list of his daily activities, explains
his lack of detail, everything can be summed up
easily in four words: sleep, work, meetings, leisure.
He's amazed at how much time he spends on leisure.
And the empty page? That's for today's activities.
He just wrote yesterday's this morning. He admits
he didn't get in all his community volunteer hours
this week, too sick, too cold, too many
addiction meetings, though he confesses
to having missed a couple of those too; his clock,
the weather, the lost list of locations and, sorry,
but he completely forgot about the Judge's order
to write a Procrastination Paper, forgot
until early this morning and then it was just too late.
He'll do it tomorrow. He's quite sure he will,
do it, tomorrow. Yes, tomorrow for sure.

Not Yet

T-shirts wrapped tight around swollen belly-
rings and back tattoos playing peek-a-boo
above sloppy gray sweats, these young women
are addicts on probation.

They must come to court every week,
report on dentist and doctor appointments,
parenting classes, birth certificates,
ID cards, health care numbers.

Necessary things now, for a parent-to-be,
but not then, not when you're an addict
not as important as the next hit
when you're working the streets.

A clean screen, applause, and a sigh of relief,
hope for the unborn who's not yet been cooked.
We pray.

This Judge

He saw me
first in the prisoners box
no place to hide, I had to stand
a derelict, trembling mess,
not much of a man.

He heard all the things
I'd done to get the stuff
that makes me feel good
helps me to forget.

When I came back from rehab
clean shaven, sober
he chose me to take notes
at the front of the courtroom.

He saw me,
looked beyond the anger
the attitude the addiction
my affliction. He helped me
to believe.

This Judge saw
in me a someone
that I had never seen.
He saw the person
I want to become.

Jacob Reports on the Recovery Centre

He says it's like an artichoke,
perhaps because it's thorny,
or maybe it's what the word evokes,
the struggle, the addict's journey.
It's not for everyone, this taste,
(increases the bile for a while)
but to discard it all as simply a waste
makes futile this present trial.

For even the artichoke has a heart,
needs to be boiled until tender,
salt in the water/wound, smarts at the start,
helps heal the liver. A spiny surrender.
So here's to the cardunculus, prickles and all.
Here's to Jacob's success with the artichoke protocol.

Feral

If the courtroom were a zoo,
the prisoner's dock a cage,
she would be the tiger
pacing the perimeter
snarling at the injustice
of her captured state.

And this older man
who has come hoping
for her release
must watch in horror
as his daughter lashes out
at those who offer help.

But this courtroom isn't a zoo,
and her prison's not a cage. It's heroin
that has her trapped. He's shocked,
doesn't recognize this wild woman
who claws at the bars
as her keepers take her away.

It's too much. He leaves
weeping for the sweet girl she was,
for her mother and her children
waiting at home. Knows now
only she can set herself free.

Biceps Curl

Hairy, tattooed, scarred, this arm
has a fist bigger than the baby's head
that lies in the crook of its brawny elbow.
Inside a bicep wider than her whole body,
a newborn sleeps, her legs smaller
than the calloused fingers that hold her
bottle, as her mother tells the Judge
she's been clean for eight months. Applause
startles the infant, but this strong arm
rocks her back to sleep,
                        today.

To Be-Come

You are the life in the belly
of that young woman in the prisoner's box.

An accidental, unwanted life, perhaps the result
of a drunken egg's encounter with some john's sperm.

You have already slept in doorways,
know the taste of heroin, felt the effects of ecstasy.

You must have struggled to stay afloat
in that viscous stew of alcohol and dope.

Today you swim in clearer waters,
a bump inside institution sweats, a promise

budding. You are a he, a she, or maybe both,
a baby, a child, an adult, a person-to-be.

We hear your cries amidst the gurgle and tick
in this courtroom, you are an insistent presence.

Fermented and floundering inside
this muddled woman. No choice. No voice.

We hear you and feel powerless.
We hear you and are humbled.

Offered a chance to beat her addiction
the young woman lays a hand on her belly.

You are the life beneath that hand,
we pray she hears you too.

Conversations with the Judge

A's blond ponytail bounces as she flies
to the front of the courtroom,
exhales her busy week to the Judge,
all in one breath, it seems,
while her bony body, her head, her hands,
twitch and bob and flutter as if a goldfinch
had come to perch in this court.

In a sweet breathless voice
she tells the court that today
has been a trying day. But,
she's not ready to talk about it
yet. Says it's big, but not so big
she can't handle it herself. Says
she's got lots of support.
Not like a few months ago.

When I would have gone out and used, but
I think I can handle it now.
I'm going to the symphony.
Hopefully my methadone dose is low
enough I'll be able to stay awake.

B's bubbly as she speaks,
reports her kids are doing well,
she hasn't had a smoke in eight days,
eighteen pounds down,
eleven months clean, due to graduate
next month but, her voice trembles
as she admits she's terrified, one month,
only one month to go. *I'm scared*
to leave this court, scared
of being without support.
I'm really scared.

C says,
*I got all uptight
Saturday night, left
the house, went to a bar. Yes,
I used but only once. It's okay,
I have lots of support. It's okay.*

She looks at the floor
and hesitantly turns away.

D's going to jail,
knows it's not where he wants to be,
not who he is anymore. He's in love,
baby on the way, but
it caught up with him,
he can't deny the devil
drug that made him
break and enter, made him
steal, made him drive a stolen car,
made him sell what he didn't use.
Too many excuses, too many bad tests.
It's too late. He'll have to do his time.

*I hope we see you back here again
when you get out,* says the Judge
as he's led away.

E got mad
when the Judge asked
for proof of attendance
at meetings, he got mad,
said he had it, just forgot it,
couldn't find it, left it behind
again this week. He got mad,
says he doesn't like
the distrust, so—he's mad.

F speaks with the Judge,
I just found out, my daughter
is skipping school, riding trains,
hanging out in the mall, just
like me. I did those things,
and now she … but I didn't get mad,
I'm proud of that. I just talked to her,
had her sign a contract. I can't
have her messing it all up for me now—
all I've been through. It's troubling
to watch your child make the same
mistakes that you once made. Knowing
where it leads. I've asked for help.
I still have so much to learn.

G's young, still pretty,
back in custody. She broke curfew,
used, was arrested, again. Tells
the Judge she'll try to do better
this time, she'll try harder
to stay in the program. She
says she wants to beat her addiction,
really wants to live clean.

But as her parole conditions are read
her eyes glaze over and she slouches
against the rail of the prisoners box,
tapping one toe and impatiently
rolling a hair elastic in her fingers, as if
she were hearing a familiar prayer,
as if she'd heard it once too often. As if—
she didn't really care.

H. If H were a wrestler,
he'd be the bad guy, all skull,
shoulders, jaw and tattoos. Tough
appearance, yet here in Drug Court
he admits he's afraid he'll mess up,
he's lonely, unfamiliar with living on the outside,
jail has been his home for too long, too often. He's lost
all his family, his friends. He's lonely,
scared, wants to go back, inside
jail for just awhile longer, later,
he says, he'll try again—
later.

I is nervous, stuttering, can't find the words.
It's her first week, first time to speak,
to explain her distress, choked up, unable
to obey the order to speak louder, can't
understand why there is laughter
at the back of the courtroom,
thinks it's about her, doesn't know
they are laughing at something
else, someone else, doesn't realize
that they aren't even listening to her.

I don't think, she sobs to the Judge,
this is the right place for me. She can't
imagine this weekly roasting.

J could be a lawyer
as he walks forward confidently
in black oxfords and well cut grey suit
with starched white shirt and tasteful tie. He could
have been, might still be—
though not today as he takes the mike
to tell the Judge of his cocaine addiction,
broken marriage, lost job. *I never thought*
it could happen to me. I just never thought.

K asserts:
I'm not too drug-affected
to be assessed, Judge. No
it's narcolepsy, see, I've
got narcolepsy, I fall asleep
everywhere, even riding a bike,
slept all the time I was in jail,
had it for six years, has to do
with working nights all my life.
Doctor's cure is uppers and I'm not
into pharmaceuticals, too many
when I was young, ruined my kidneys.
my bladder, my liver … what
is my addiction? Well, Judge,
it's crack, yeah I know it's an upper,
but see, I don't do heroin
look at my arms. Besides that
Detox is a bad place to live—
not good for my asthma.

L admits: *It's been seven months.*
I guess I'm a slow learner.
It's hard for me to believe
the team is not here to put me back
in jail. Hard to believe
they're really trying
to keep me out. They're breaking me
down, little by little. It's been years
and years, so much betrayal, so much distrust.

M stands up:
Your honour, as a mother I must thank you
for bringing my daughter back
to us. We lost her for a year
to crystal meth. Now
not only do we have her,
we have her baby daughter.
This time you saved two
lives—maybe more, now
she's gone back to school,
plans to become a doctor, to help
others who, like her, have lost their way.

N attests:
She'd probably be dead. My girlfriend,
she got sick last week, couldn't get out of bed,
so hot, she couldn't breathe, coughed blood.
I kept my head, got her to a hospital.
They say I saved her life. Just think,
back in our using days, we'd both
be out there on the street, and—
she'd probably be dead.

O observes:
I have to focus on what's important
to me, that's my children. My addiction,
my criminal behaviour took me away
from them. I don't need
to be in jail. I have a disease
and there is a cure. I'm learning.

P is elated:
I'm twenty-six this week
and I finally got my driver's license.
Oh yeah, I always knew how,
used to steal cars, drove them away, but
now I don't have to worry when
I pull up beside a police car.

Q is really disturbed today. *So many*
dirty screens. So many just playing
the game. Don't they know,
this program, the team, they're there
for us, such a shame to waste it.

R: *I grew up a street girl, came from*
three different skid rows. Learned
not to trust. Didn't believe
I was worth saving. You have saved
two lives, mine and my son's.
It's a ripple effect that can't be explained.

S: *Today,*
I'm a totally different person
than I was two years ago
when I entered this program, still working
on opening myself up
to different experiences, but
I didn't realize
how much I've developed.
I'm happy
with myself, proud
of what I've done,
and who I am
today.

T: *I've spent most of my life in jail.*
I don't know no other way,
don't know what to do, what to say,
how to act. Those guys inside, they talk
about drugs and all that shit—excuse
my language—I don't want that any more, I want
to get outta jail, get off the stuff. I'm over thirty,
have nothing to show for it. I wanna
learn another way to live.

U: *I'm one year clean today,*
don't like to boast,
but that meth, it holds people hostage,
hard to break away. I couldn't
have done it without your help.
So I'm telling it here
want others to know
it can be done, want
them to know that
Drug Courts work.

V's graduating today.
It's possible, you know,
just do what they want
you to do. It's possible.

W: *I used. Met up with old friends.*
Lied. Missed appointments,
didn't phone the team.
Learned. You'll never beat addiction
if you're only willing to go half way—
You have to change everything!

X: *I'd rather bike and skateboard,*
but not running, you see, it's like—
a thing this—like
running from the police.

I don't do that anymore

Y: *Living in the river valley*
and watching the snow melt
off my sleeping bag … it's
just not something I want
to ever experience again!

Z: *I'm not going to say that it's been easy*
because it's not. It's probably the hardest thing
I've ever done. No one can do this alone.
If you think you can, you're in trouble.
Ask for what you need. This program does work.
Now I don't have to walk into the community
and have them turn their backs on me.
I can't say enough about this program.
It saved my life!

Courtroom Waltz

The little girl dances, spins round and round,
boots pointed blunt, as her mother waltzes her lies,
cocaine, yes, again. Once, only once.
slow, quick, quick, slow, quick, quick …

When her mother cries, the child closes her eyes,
pirouettes, a butterfly, thin arms flung wide
as if wanting to fly. Four years old, whispering,
wriggling, waiting for the end of this show and tell.

No Rainbow Here Today

In Too Deep

Everyone can see
she's in trouble, weighted down
with amphetamines and cocaine—
not the lifesavers she'd hoped for.
She's stopped eating again.
Now she struggles to stay afloat.

How did she get
into this deep water?
Clean for a year,
she'd learned how to swim,
begun to trust her body, nourish it,
even like it a little. She was
making wiser choices. She was.

Now she's surfaced for the third time,
malnourished, drug-saturated,
no struggle left,
sinking—
as those who care scurry
to find any kind of lifeline
long enough to reach her, strong
enough to pull her out.

It seems hopeless.
Detox overflowing, no beds
at the hospital, no room
in residential rehab, no place, no space,
no help for this very sick human being.
She is slowly going under,
her outstretched hand
is all that's left.

It is the Judge
who finally comes to the rescue,
throws out
the only life preserver left.

I'm going to jail! Oh my God,
I've never been to jail.
I thought you guys were supposed to help me!

She cries
as the rope wraps
around her wrists
to pull her in.
They lock her up—
dry her out—
save her life—
              this time.

A Wife's Lament

See. That's my husband talking to the Judge,
again. He's promising to change his ways.
He lies. I've heard them all many times before.
It's hard when coke is your mistress, too hard for this man,
a good man, once, good husband and father, lost.
Lost to the streets, he's become a slave to his needs.
I don't know why I'm here today. His needs
should no longer matter. Hurt and betrayed, I judged
him, found him guilty long ago. He's lost
to me. I can no longer tolerate the way
he abuses us. My children suffer, a mutant man,
angry, slovenly, absent, not like before

he had that accident on the job, before
he backed over the little boy, before his need
to forget turned him onto drugs. This man
was respected, in demand, competent to judge
the work of those who came to learn his ways
with wood, how he could find its soul. All lost.

Wood's secrets whittled down generations, lost
in a blurred city jungle. He no longer cares for
his family, will do anything to make the pain go away,
lives now only to feed that ceaseless need
to tame those hungry ghosts. But even on judgement
day I fear I'll still feel love for this man.

Why do I always come running back? Man,
I really can't say. I thought that love was lost
three years ago, the day he beat me, fudged
my bank card, emptied my wallet, left before
I woke, fragrantly painted in blood, needed
thirty-six stitches, a safe house. What a way

to end a marriage. Yet I drove this highway
today to come to this court, to see if the man
on the phone has really changed, repented. I need
to see it for myself. So much is lost.
It can never be what it was before
and yet, here I am against my better judgement.

I will weigh the evidence against what I've lost,
find I can't ignore what that man's done before.
I need to keep my sanity. His, I'll leave for the Judge.

       Or, will I weigh the evidence against what's been lost.
       If this man still has the soul I loved before,
       I may decide I need to plead with the Judge.

Second Chance

Your daughter slouches
in the front row of the courtroom,
thick dark curls fall forward
                    cover her frail face.

You are her father. A warrant
brought her here to Drug Court,
hoping for a second chance.
                    you pray for a miracle.

You watch your wife, instructed
by the Judge to come forward,
to sit beside your daughter,
                    hold her upright.

You see your adult daughter, slump
against her mother, unable to stay
awake, so weak, so faint. You loathe
                    her needled wants.

You are powerless
over the addiction that has captured your child,
devastated your wife. Now you both must watch her
                    handcuffed, taken into custody.

You leave the courtroom feeling—
relief? Perhaps. She's off the streets, safe—
for now. Yet one never knows, one never
                    really knows.

Tripping Over a Cornerstone

Honesty is the cornerstone on which this drug rehabilitation treatment court is based.

He's going back to jail, again,
seems a nice enough guy,
abandoned at birth,
raised on the reserve.

He seems a nice enough guy.
Abused by his uncle,
raised on the reserve,
got lost in the maze of city streets.

Abused by his uncle,
he gets by on charm, booze and lies,
lost in the maze of city streets,
wrecked his lungs on bad weed.

He always got by on charm, booze and lies.
Don't think like a victim, his psychologist warns.
Wrecked his lungs on bad weed,
now he drags an oxygen tank to Drug Court.

Don't think like a victim, his psychologist warns.
Even house arrest can't contain this addict,
dragging his oxygen tank to court,
thinks honesty a foreign word.

Even house arrest can't contain this addict,
abandoned at birth.
For him honesty is a foreign word,
he's going back to jail again.

Had a Relapse

I confess, did one line of cocaine.
The choice was there for me:
use or not use.

In jail for five months, I was angry,
a resentful man, missed my children,
my wife.

Thought I had it handled.
But living with my family again
it's been hard.

My stepsons are hiding booze,
talking back, missing school.
We're in debt.

I can't help. For some reason
I wanted an easy way out.
Found that it wasn't.

I feel terrible. This program preaches honesty.
At least I was honest. Phoned my P.O.
right away. I'm trying,

want to do the right things, working out,
going to meetings, getting a sponsor.
It's damn difficult.

I want to offer so much
but I don't
have much to offer.

No Rainbow Here Today

Grey: this man who cowers
mutely before the Judge, smoky
head drooped, shoulders hunched,
hands limp at his sides, drained—
of all colour, all song. Spirit coated
with powder, suffocating,
power of crack, plunder of cocaine.
His face a mask, frozen in defeat.

Blue: the young woman who stands
at his side and speaks to the Judge
about her father. A good man, once,
when she was younger, never been in trouble, never
broken the law before. Before he changed.
She can't explain
what led him down the path to this.
Doesn't understand
why he can't go back, turn it around.
She's afraid for him. In jail or free,
she sees disaster, either way.
She pleads, *Don't give up
on him*, her voice breaks, her sobs
echo through the courtroom.

Pink: the child in the second row,
her dress, her soother, the bow
in her blond curly hair. She's just
climbed onto Gramma's lap, distracted
by a ring of keys, a bottle, a cookie, too young,
perhaps, at two, to know the why
of her mother's tears, her grandfather's
plight. Her life still so fresh, so new.

Yellow: the woman who holds
the child, holds in, holds on, her husband,
hooked, maimed, broken. Her love
in ashes, her anger fuelled
by lame excuses. She's come here
again and again. This time
too jaundiced to speak. Shamed
by her husband's defeat, she bleeds
at her daughter's pain, cannot justify
this witness, her own granddaughter.
A guilty plea, the plain facts, the sentencing, last
brittle leaves of hope crushed.

Black and white: this courtroom, devoid
of windows, flowers, plants, sombre, silent,
somnolent, sad. A rescued sparrow
has fallen from the tree again, fallen
down, fallen back into the storm.
There's no rainbow here today.

Your Honour

Memory becomes a festering wound. ~ Nietzsche

I've always been a drunk,
me, my mother's youngest son.
Now I'm dry and she's dying.
At eighty-two, her heart is battered,
my brother's early death,
my bootless, bottle-filled life.

> *Wednesday afternoon and here am I again*
> *in front of this woman. She wants*
> *me to talk, well I can do that.*
> *I'm a good talker, have BS'd my way out lotsa*
> *trouble, lots and lotsa trouble.*

In the beginning vodka
was my favourite, easiest
to hide in my morning coffee,
After I lost my job, my wife
kicked me out. Then
it didn't much matter.

> *Ah yes, my old lady, what a case*
> *she was. Always naggin', groanin',*
> *phonin'. Didn't like my smokin',*
> *my drinkin'. Well, I quit my job,*
> *she ain't gettin' nothin' out'a me. Nothin',*

Newly sober I find myself
in a slough of regrets.
I'd like to wade out of the past
but I'm caught in its muck. Plagued,
by regret. It's the mosquito in the dark,
the thistle in my sock, the bee in my belly.

Shoulda, coulda said, a crab in my crotch,
though a beer in my belly would do.
Sure could use a beer. Bet one beer
wouldn't mess up my screen. Can't
chance it. I've got this lady charmed—
always could charm the ladies.

Oh, this clean life, both wonderful
and difficult. A test. The news,
my Mom, upset with me, my failings—
her failing. Haven't seen her in years,
but I'm so deep in debt, still a threat
at the border. I cannot get to her.

Goddamn conditions! Listen Lady
you could help me out here. Sure
would be nice to skip out'a here
and cross the border. I don't know
how much longer I can last
without some booze.

Can't go back, can't change the past,
I'm stressed, fear being alone. Regret
forces me to look behind. Once I had the chance
to be a parent. Messed that up too,
though it helps me understand my mother's pain,
why she can't forget, can't forgive.

Had a witch for a mother, witch, bitch,
such a snitch, called the cops
when I was twelve, had me arrested,
wouldn't pay my bail, spent
the night in jail, said it was a lesson,
didn't want me to fail.

Wish I could see her, want to show her
I'm trying hard to move forward,
to look ahead, want to tell her I won't
let regret hold me back, weight me down,
I'm determined, I can, I will,
I must, try again—harder this time,

> *This time, I'm in a bind. One gulp*
> *of red wine could bring me down.*
> *Hey you, don't you judge.*
> *Why that frown? Can't you see*
> *my mouth, it's smiling!*

Harder to restore this abandoned house,
throw out all regret, build new
memories, live the rest of my life
on this Sober Road.

Consequences

It's the half-inch dagger sticking out of his lower lip one notices first. It's hard to guess the age of this young man with jet black hair gelled and spiked so high on his head. He's wearing the uniform of the street, a black and white print hoodie and jeans hung so low on the hips that the crotch reaches his knees almost tripping him as he walks to the front of the courtroom.

He's the random man. It seems like every week he tells the Judge how he likes to do random things. It's the way he says it; *Ran—dom* letting the word slide off his tongue so slowly and in two separate parts, starting with a high *ran* and ending on a low drawn out *dummm*. Then he repeats it again as if he's just learned the word and needs to let it get comfortable on his tongue, *Yeah, ran-dommm*. and he lets out a short snorting *Hah* as he stuffs his hands into his pockets to hitch up his jeans as he turns around to see if anyone else thinks he's funny. If encouraged he'll continue, *I took off my shirt last week when it was -30 and danced bare-chested in Churchill Square. Now that's ran-dommm!*

Arrested on charges related to his addictions he's been offered a second chance at freedom, Drug Court. So far he's spent six weeks in a residential drug rehabilitation program and now resides in a residence for addicts in the city. He's been given strict conditions to attend NA meetings, take urine screens, do community service and be in court every Wednesday afternoon to report his progress to the Judge.

Went paint balling on Sunday without my shirt and now my chest's all stained. Now that's kind of ran-domm except that it hurt too much so I put on overalls. Now some of the cuts are infected and I had to go to the doctor. That's why I'm so late. But you have to admit it was pretty RAN-DOMM!

He's been coming to court now for two months. His conversations with the Judge are always a little juvenile. He often looks for approval from his fellow participants in the courtroom when he talks about being bored and looking to do more crazy, random things.

A group of us went to the University visited a place with lots of bugs. Pretty ran-dom eh? Some of the girls were like, icky, but I kind of like bugs.

Nothing random today in Drug Court though, as he stands before the Judge. He's been found out and now he admits to his deceit. Says he thought that he could wash out the ecstasy and mushrooms he took on Friday over the weekend. He didn't think that the urine screen would give him away.

They say that kids who live on the streets don't grow up, that they stay the age they were when they left home. This young man in adult court is nineteen but he's still fourteen in his ways. One has to wonder about all the drugs, the crystal meth he used to sell, the ecstasy and mushrooms he took last weekend, wonder what damage has already been done to his brain.

You could have died! said the Judge. *Do you understand?*

The IF Factor

As if he'd never
forged a money order,
held fraudulent credit cards,
possessed break-in tools,

As if he'd never impersonated
another to open a mailbox,
take their mail, passports,
birth certificates.

As if he'd never
invaded bank accounts,
transferred funds,
withdrawn thousands of dollars.

As if he wasn't
a drug addict, an ex-con,
who used his charm, his criminal
smarts to feed his habit.

If only while on probation,
five-months clean, he hadn't
complained to Drug Treatment Court
about his difficulties,
getting credit, being trusted.

If only he hadn't told the Judge
that his court conditions
(no cell phone, no computer)
meant it was the court's fault
he couldn't find a job.

If only he hadn't been
driving a known drug dealer's car
when stopped by the police,
with false license, fake name,
cell phone, stash in the trunk.

If only days after meeting
with the TD Bank manager
to apologize and show them how
he'd hacked into their system.
he hadn't been arrested—
again, wasn't there in the prisoners box
on Wednesday afternoon, wasn't
expelled from Drug Court, now
will be tried,
sent back to jail.

What if he'd stayed the course,
kept all his conditions, found a job
that didn't require computer
or cell phone, cut off his criminal
connections, stayed drug free
for a year, graduated, cleared
of all charges, free?

What if he'd gone back to school
studied computer sciences, developed
a computer program that would destroy
all viruses at their source, invented
a thumbprint password, a sure-proof
way to eradicate identity theft?

What if he'd used his intelligence
and charisma for diplomacy? What
would he have done for world peace?

If not him, then who?
If not now, then when?

A Thorny Love

She's burnt out, done,
her health suffers,
she says she can't do it,
can't keep taking him in,
can't look after him anymore,
can't be his keeper. No matter how much

she loves this young man
she raised after her daughter died.
She still cares, wants to protect him,
which is why she's back again
in this courtroom when he's called
up before the Judge.

His lawyer tries to explain
away his dirty screens, his second
ejection from rehab, tries
to keep him out of jail, but
this young man burnt all his bridges,
there's no place left to go.

She thinks back to the little boy
she bathed, dressed, hugged,
nursed through illnesses. She remembers,
holding him on her lap
as she read to him each night,
tucked him in, left on the light.

He was always afraid of monsters,
afraid of being caught, afraid
of the dark, nightmares
haunted him. Too young
for his father's abuse. Still young
when she rescued him.

When did it change? How did they
get to this point? She's too sick, too tired,
too old, no longer able to kiss it all better.
How many times can she forgive,
his lying, his scheming,
his stealing—from her?

She's taken him in again and again,
believed him when he said he wants to change,
wants to live a different life, needs another
chance. But he's caught
in the claws of crystal meth,
can't seem to free himself.

Today she vows to stay strong
while the Judge explains to him
that since he no longer has a place
to stay, he's going back into custody. Maybe,
just maybe he'll learn a lesson, maybe
this time he'll try harder to beat his addiction.

She watches as he strides angrily
to the prisoner's dock. Her jaw is set.
She says it's for the best, says she won't
take him back again, say's she just can't—
wouldn't, couldn't, shouldn't—
but then again, if he promises … how can she not?

From Prison Garb to Business Suit

Graduation

The young man at the back of the courtroom fiddles with his tie, stretches his chin forward and up, out of the starched white collar of his shirt. He unbuttons his jacket, tugs it down, buttons it up again, checks the zipper on his fly, runs a hand through his freshly cut hair, shrugs one shoulder then the other, rubs fingers against his clean shaven cheek before going back to straighten his tie again.

I smile as I watch him fiddle and twitch. I've seen him here almost every Wednesday afternoon dressed in blue jeans, a clean t-shirt and black leather jacket. I've watched him come forward shyly to report his progress or his failures to the Judge. I've joined the applause at the report of every clean drug screen.

He drops his head and his face reddens as the drug treatment team list off the reasons why he's ready for graduation. The two years of weekly clean screens, the hours spent volunteering at Meals on Wheels, the large number of AA meetings attended, all the appointments kept, the courses taken, how he waited until he was sure he could handle his addiction himself.

Though I've never spoken to him or he to me, there are tears as I watch the Judge make her way cautiously down the stairs from the dais to present him with his graduation certificate. I am part of an expectant silence—everyone holding their breath—as he bends down to be hugged by this tiny, gowned woman.

It's his turn now to speak. Handsome, tall, well dressed and now, so resolute, he stands, head held high, looks up at the Judge as he places his right hand over his heart, clears his throat and in a voice hoarse with emotion, says, "Gratitude is the heart's memory."

> Sunny day
> a young man's reflection
> smiles

With Honours

Emily graduated today, pleaded guilty to drug charges laid eighteen months ago, received a non-custodial sentence, then, was hugged by that same Judge.

Emily graduated today after 181 AA meetings, 81 clean drug screens, 300 hours of community service, and many more hours of counselling and courses on parenting, anger management, drug relapse prevention.

Emily graduated today, then turned and apologized to her four children present for what she has put them through, for having made them temporary wards of the government, separated, in foster homes, while their mother was addicted, a criminal, jailed, unfit to parent.

Emily graduated today, eight months after she gained back custody of her children, eight months after she proved she can weather the storms that come with being a single parent on probation, a recovering addict trying to meet all the strict conditions of a judicial drug recovery treatment program.

Emily graduated today, said she didn't want this day to come, didn't want to leave the security of Drug Court for it was here that she'd learned patience, learned honesty, learned to believe that she could heal, could become someone who could help others, wants to be an elementary teacher or an addictions counsellor.

Emily graduated today from Drug Treatment Court equipped with new tools to control those hungry ghosts who still sometimes whisper to her in the dark when she's lonely or frightened, though now she knows there are people to call, places to go, healthy things she can do to feed the emptiness.

Emily graduated today, left the courtroom with her family. Five people walked out that door. Five people who have been given a second chance at life.

Emily graduated today. Her thirteen-year-old daughter, the one who her mother prays will not make the same mistakes, her pretty, independent daughter, holds her baby brother in her arms and listens. She listens, but does she really hear?

Testimony

My name is Molly and I'm an addict.

I can't tell you when it began. My parents put alcohol in my bottle to make me sleep. Both were addicts, our house, a crack shack. Sometimes I didn't get a bath for weeks, was always hungry, often only bread and beer for supper. Then the abuse. I never learned how to live, what to do with my days, what was normal. Alcohol was my gateway drug. I found cocaine at twenty-five. When my daughter was born I didn't want to leave her in her crib. I was so afraid of losing her. When they took her from me I went back to the ways of the street, tried to commit suicide, twice, went to jail, got out, got high, back in jail, got out, got high. That was my circle of life. Until the day I was ushered into the prisoners' box to watch another woman graduate from Drug Court. I wanted that. I wanted it bad, begged to get in. Drug Court saved my life. I'll be one year clean next week. I've got my daughter back. I have a job and a place of my own for the first time in my life. I'm 40 years old and now I know that I can be whatever I want to be.

My name is Molly and I'm an addict whose life matters.

From Prison Garb to Business Suit

Who is this dapper man in the dark business suit,
with starched shirt, striped tie and leather shoes
standing here at the front of the courtroom
in conversation with the Judge?

He's not young, his hair thins, though he's lean and fit.
Articulate too as he introduces his friends to the court,
tells of their kindness to a drunk on the corner,
how they offered him lodging, gave him a job.

Can this be the same man who, eight months ago,
stood in the dock, unshaven, unkempt, dressed
in navy sweats, homeless, charged with theft, the same man
who pled guilty, then eloquently asked for help?

He's always had a way with words. Reported weekly
to the Judge, spoke of his mother's illness, their
unfinished business, his regrets, his loneliness, his job,
the hard daily climb, how it got easier, how he got better.

Who is this person who graduates from Drug Court today
a free man? He's the same, yet, not the same.
For that man in prison garb only had a past,
this man in suit and tie, this man has earned a future.

Cowboy Courage

It's Thursday morning in Calgary's flashy new steel and glass courthouse. The Stampede's over but here there's still reason to celebrate. It's graduation day in Courtroom 505. This man's no cowboy but he's shown he's got the guts to ride a bucking bronco through the agony of withdrawal and win. It hasn't been easy. It's hard enough to last eight seconds, let alone fourteen months. But he'd already had a fifteen year struggle with the rankest of stock. And though there's no silver buckle at the end of this ride, his prize is the rest of his life. He's got his health, a home, and a job. He's going to use what he learned while hooked on the horns of crystal meth, heroin and Listerine to help those who are still trying to survive the spurs and burrs of an addict's life on the streets. This man doesn't want to forget that ride, the many falls, the pain of landing, of being trod upon again and again. But today he's in the winners' circle with his family, his friends and his colleagues. Today, it's white Stetsons off for his cowboy courage.

sobriety
off the horse
the pinch of new boots

The Circumstances

It was a dog that brought me down
in the end. I've still got the scars
on my arms to prove it. Don't blame the dog,
I was already down, way down, stealing
from Laundromats to feed my cocaine habit.
I suppose I could have run
but I had nowhere else to go.
I was homeless, begging in the streets,
a mess of a man. Besides, the police had a gun.

My mother died when I was five. At six
my father stole me from a foster home. Took me
across the country. A drunk and a thief, he was
jailed when I was nine. Left me alone, left me
to fend for myself. I managed to go to school for a while,
slept in stairwells, did whatever I had to do. In June
they picked me up, took me back to Saskatoon. I ran away
often, was caught, brought back, beaten
until my spirit was flat like a pricked balloon.

It was a horse that saved me,
an old palomino mare named Rayla Jane.
She was the one who let me cry. Me,
the son of an army man, who wasn't allowed to cry
even when my mother died. Rayla Jane let me
bury my face in her mane. It's true,
I sobbed out years of sorrow. It was that horse
whose warmth I sought when I first began
to feel again. Judge, I'm ready to start anew.

I'll soon be forty, spent
almost twenty of those years in jail, committed
more crimes than I can count. Shame's a harsh bit,
addiction a heavy saddle. I've dropped them both
along the way. It took a dog, a patient horse, and now
this woman, who has bravely consented to be my wife.
I'm proof that Drug Court works. So, I want to say
to those who still struggle: You've been offered a second chance.
A winning ticket. Don't waste your years like I did.

The Music of the Ordinary

He smiles as he shovels snow off the sidewalk,
tosses it into the yard, then stops to lean
on the shovel, show his face to the sky,
wanting to feel, just feel snow's touch
on his skin, its prick, the melt, the drip.
He doesn't mind snow this late in April. He's happy
not to be inside, looking out windows—
behind bars.

He studies each flake as it lands on his sleeve,
shaped like the doilies his grandmother made.
One good memory floats like a water lily,
on the murky depths of his past. Heartache burns.
He tugs his toque farther down to cover his ears
digs another shovelful of snow off the walk.
The strength of his own body surprises him
these days. He still can't believe its get-up-and-go,
how well it runs when fuelled with food. Not alcohol,
not drugs.

Snow swirls around him as he sweeps the steps
to the house—his house now. It's warm inside.
A pot of soup waits on the stove.
There's a second-hand table, chairs, a radio,
battered sofa—a bed. A bed
with a pillow, clean sheets, comforter.
Such a change from last summer
when he slept in a cardboard box near the river,
begged on the street.

He doesn't mind that snow blows in his face. He's happy
to be doing this ordinary thing. Earlier
today, as he washed dishes, up to his elbows
in warm, soapy water, he realized joy—
yes, joy, in the washing, the drying, the putting away
of these few dishes into his once bare cupboard.
High on the everyday.

He hesitates at the back door. Snow muffles
the sounds of the city, casts halos around
each street light. He admires the way it
adorns every tree, every fence post, fire hydrant,
garbage can, how it erases old footprints, makes room
for new ones, how it creates a fresh page overnight.
He wonders if recovery, if going straight, if being clean
can do the same for him? He wants to believe
it can—that he can—that he will—
this time. God willing.

He's got a record, got a label. It's not musical,
his list of crimes, his time served in jail. He's an addict.
That's scary, but this,
this storm, this snow, these warm clothes, this house,
the soup, the dishes, the bed, his body—oh boy!
He just wants to sing—sing along to the music,
this music of the everyday,
the music of the ordinary.

A Shuffling of Christmas Quotes

First holiday I've enjoyed in a long time.
I actually cooked a turkey
and people got to see me sober,
actually present for the presents.
My father even came with me to a meeting.

*

To be perfectly honest
it was not all good,
a 50-50 holiday.
I went a little loopy
used a lot of stuff.
spent the holidays in detox.

*

Except for the ones
I spent in jail
this is the first one
I've been sober
not on the couch
sleeping it off—

*

My sister danced
around my bed,
my family happy,
love me sober,
not out
looking for another hit.

*

Went off my medication
hit the streets
surprised how far I fell,
like before, before, long before,
shocked at where crack will take me.

*

Got a gift card.
felt like drinking
remembered all the things my mother taught me
so I just removed myself from the situation,
different spending New Years alone.
It feels like I'm in the right place.
Bought myself a new T.V.
the first one I actually own legally,
got a warranty card and all.

*

Visited my parents.
They love having their daughter back.
It's a first, a sober Christmas.
So happy that I'm clean,
had a clean screen today
the best gift I got this year.
Did I mention
Christmas was awesome?

Courtroom Videography

It's a happy buzz that we hear when the camcorder turns on. It's situated today at the back right hand side of Edmonton's Courtroom 267. Videotaping not allowed, of course, in a courtroom except when it's through the lens in the eye of an observer whose films are simply reels of words.

At first all we see is the black and white of pen, paper and the back of the wooden bench in front. Then the camera moves up and onto the squinting face of a newborn baby wrapped in flannel. He is being rocked in his mother's arms and, for a moment, so are we, before the camera moves over the heads of the people in the next four rows to focus on the prisoner's dock at the far right. Four men and one woman dressed in navy prison garb sit on one straight wooden bench fenced in and surrounded on either end by sober-faced, blue uniformed security guards. The men are slouched on the bench eyeing the crowd for a familiar face, while the young woman has dropped her head to hide behind her long straggly hair. The camera recedes to catch the almost full courtroom in various stages of devouring chocolate and vanilla cupcakes, a rare treat, we hear the Judge explain, due to one of the participant's birthday falling on a court day.

The picture now settles on an attractive red haired woman standing in the centre of the courtroom holding her new graduation certificate. She turns to speak: *In the past fourteen months I've grown into a person I never expected to be. I've had the chance to get to know me. Now it's up to me. I've got my children back, reconnected with my family, moved into a house, got a summer job, and plan to go back to school in September. I'd like you to meet my mother.*

At the back of the courtroom we see an older well-dressed woman wipe her eyes. When asked if she'd like to speak, she can only sob, *Thank you for giving us our daughter back,* and reaches for the hand of the smiling man beside her.

A name is called and the camera pans across the rows to a young man. As he stands we see a glimpse of his patterned boxer shorts before he reaches with his right hand to pull up his baggy jeans. Then a close-up of his black high-tops as he walks to the mike situated on a wooden podium near the front of the courtroom. We hear the Judge ask him about his week. We see him pull a small day-timer from his back pocket, fumble to open it. We see his hands tremble; hear the ripple of pages as he nervously fingers through the book. There's sharp intake of breath as he begins: *I went to five meetings last week. Then last Thursday I got fitted for a Tux for my brother's wedding. Hard to believe that just a while ago I was living in a tent. I've been clean for eight months today.*

Loud applause as the camera flashes over the full courtroom. A woman dressed in a suit and heels sits at the left of the two wide oak tables just in front of the dais. At the table on the right is a slim man in a grey suit and tie with kind eyes and a non-threatening manner. Beside him sits a young woman, a hoodie hiding her blue hair. She's writing in a scribbler. We guess that one is a representative from the Drug Court team and the other, one of the participants. The gowned court clerk sits at a raised desk facing the courtroom.

High up at the front, just below a crest of Alberta, sits the Judge in black robes and blue sash. She smiles as another name is called and a young woman with a long curly ponytail carries her infant son to the front where she balances him on the podium so that she can read from her datebook. The child reaches out and grabs at the mike, making a loud screeching noise, and the image flips quickly to a big tattooed man sitting apart at the back left side of the courtroom next to a stroller. He's smiling as the woman reports, *I only got to two meetings this week, but I finished all my community service work at Meals on Wheels and I began the relapse prevention course and, last Friday, I took my son to the doctor's for his shot and the doctor said that he is one of the strongest babies he's ever seen.*

The applause at the report of her clean screen startles her son and he begins to cry but is quickly soothed when returned to his father's waiting arms.

Again we're aware of the expectant hum, an upbeat kind of silence that seems unique to this courtroom. The camera captures an older man as he stands and shuffles slowly to the front, head down, shoulders bowed. This man looks different than the rest of the participants. His jeans are torn and stained, his plaid shirt hangs half out, half in and buttons seem to be missing. *"Have you got something to tell me?* we hear the Judge ask. He reaches up to scratch at his unshaven face and wipe his eyes before speaking. The hum in courtroom is hushed, still, uneasy. The man takes a deep breath and sighs. *I used. Over the weekend. An old friend came to town. He brought some stuff. I could have said no, but I didn't. After I felt so bad, I phoned my probation officer, told him. I know it was wrong. I don't know why I did it. I really don't want to go back to that old life. I'd like another chance.* For the first time he looks up at the Judge and the expression on his face is one of relief as he hears.

You were honest, this program is founded on honesty. You'll get another chance but this time, make a different choice.

The man seems taller as we watch him walk back to his seat. We see a younger man beside him reach over to shake his hand and a blond woman behind bends forward to squeeze his shoulder. Two men in front turn around to say something, perhaps words of comfort as his face turns from grim to grin.

Now the camera tracks over to the right side of the courtroom where a tall shy man is getting to his feet. As he stands we note his short hair cut, the pressed pants, the shirt and tie. At the Judge's welcoming invitation he reluctantly moves to the mike.

I just came back for my friend's graduation. Yes, I'm still running with the alumni group but not as often now that I've got a job. I'm working at Safeway for the summer but I've been accepted into the welding program at NAIT for the fall.

And what, the Judge asks, *do you want to tell these people here who are still in the program?*

Hang in there, he tells the courtroom, *it's worth it, all those conditions, all those screens, all these Wednesdays, it's worth it all.*

The hands on the brass clock on the far wall indicate 5:30. The clerk announces, *Court is adjourned.* A collective sigh, the stomping of feet, as everyone stands, a flash of black and blue exiting through the oak door at the front of the courtroom and the video cam is turned off.

Notes

Notes

Page 15: Gabor Maté: *In the Realm of Hungry Ghosts*. Knopf, Canada, 2008.

Page 16: Carolyn Forché, "Twentieth Century Poetry of Witness". *American Poetry Review* 22.22 (March-April 1993), 17.

Page 22: "All Rise" is a found poem from the official program of the National Association of Drug Court Professionals 16th Annual Drug Court Training Conference in Boston, June 2-5, 2010.

Page 23 : Thanks to Robin Cuff, executive director of Toronto Drug Treatment Court, for the words to the found poem "Why Use?".

Page 26: "Addiction" was inspired by "Sleep" by Elizabeth Tomes.

Page 28 : The quote that precedes "The Addict's Mask" is by Mary Oliver from *Swan*, p.51. Beacon Press, 2010.

Page 33: "Drug Treatment Court" was *found* in the Edmonton Journal Thursday Jan. 17/08: "Drug court gives addicts hope".

Page 42: "This Place You Call Drug Court" was inspired by Lorna Crozier's "The New Poem" in *Inventing the Hawk*. McClelland & Stewart Inc., 1992.

Page 78: The quote in "Tripping Over a Cornerstone" is one that I heard over and over in every Drug Treatment Court that I visited.

Biography

Diane Buchanan has written numerous pieces that have appeared in anthologies and journals, and has published two collections of poetry: *Ask Her Anything* and *Between the Silences*, which was a finalist for the Acorn-Plantos Award for People's Poetry. She has lived in and around Edmonton all her life. A retired nurse, her interest and empathy for people continue to inform her writing.